ST EDMUNDSBURY CATHEDRAL

Contents

Above:
The west front of the cathedral on Angel Hill.

Right:
The Jubilee Cross was given in 1964 by the Readers of the diocese. Its design incorporates a crown of arrows, recalling St Edmund, and the arms of the bishopric.

A Welcome from the Provost

Suffolk is often referred to as *Selig Suffolk* – holy Suffolk. At the heart of its holiness was that great centre of medieval pilgrimage, the Abbey of Bury, dedicated to the memory of St Edmund, the martyred 9th century King of the East Angles. Today I extend a warm welcome to pilgrims of the 20th century who come to St Edmundsbury Cathedral, the Mother Church of Suffolk and an inheritor of the ministry of the abbey. I hope you will find a sense of peace as you walk around – for here are stones hallowed by centuries of prayer and worship. Through the ministry of our chaplains you can be touched by their pastoral care and concern. In our architecture and stained glass you may well sense the reality of God – his almighty presence pervades everywhere.

Enjoy your visit – may you be changed by it.

1065–98	St Denis's Church built.
1121–48	St Denis's Church demolished; replaced by a church, dedicated to St James.
*c.*1390–1402	New chancel built.
1503	Work began on the new nave of St James's.
1711	New chancel built.
1862–4	New high-pitch roof built over the nave.
1865–9	Another new chancel built.
1914	Diocese of St Edmundsbury and Ipswich created. St James's Church became a cathedral.
1960–1	Porch and first part of cloisters built.
1970	New choir and crossing completed.
1990	New cathedral centre and song school opened.

Left and inset:
The decorated ceilings of the choir and transepts were designed by Stephen Dykes Bower and completed in 1970. It is easy to forget that many medieval churches when newly built were bright with painted decoration, highlighted with gilding. At Bury, the spirit of medieval decoration has been revived and adapted to great effect.

A Saint's Resting Place

'Lord, I have loved the habitation of thy house and the place where thine honour dwelleth.'

Right:
This stained glass representation of St Edmund is from the south side of the nave. St Edmund is shown in the traditional way, holding an arrow.

Bede, in his *Ecclesiastical History*, tells us that in about AD 630, Sigeberht, a king of the East Angles, set up a monastery, to which he hoped to retire. Later writers identified the location as Bedericesworth, the old name of Bury St Edmunds. Archaeologists confirm that people were living on the abbey site by this date.

However, in 869, another king of the East Angles, Edmund, met his death at the hands of the Danes. History has little to say of him, but within a few years of his death he came to be regarded as a saint and many legends grew up about him. He is usually represented in art holding an arrow, as his earliest biography tells us that he was tied to a tree and shot at by the Danes with the result that he looked like a porcupine. It also says that St Edmund's severed head was separated from his body and when his people found it, it was being guarded by a ferocious wolf, an incident depicted on the Bishop's throne.

It is often said that Hoxne was the place where St Edmund was martyred, but Abbo, who first wrote down the story of St Edmund's life in the 10th century, states that he died at a place called Haeglesdun (modern form, 'Hellsdon'). A place of this name exists near Norwich, but various pieces of evidence indicate that a more likely location is a field called Hellsdon at Bradfield St Clare, about 8 miles from Bury St Edmunds. There was also a manor in this parish called Sutton Hall, and Archdeacon Hermann, who wrote a life of St Edmund at Bury in the last years of the 11th century, said that the martyr was buried first at Sutton. These and other indications point to Bradfield St Clare as a likely site for the death of St Edmund, but more evidence is needed.

Given that Bedericesworth was a royal site with an ancient religious foundation, if St Edmund did die at Bradfield St Clare, there is little wonder that, in about 900, his body was brought here. In 945, another King Edmund, who regarded the saint as his kinsman, gave the monks who cared for his shrine a tract of land. This became Bury St Edmunds.

Soon after the year 1000 the Danish attacks began again and in 1010 St Edmund's body had to be taken to London for safety. The sudden death in 1014 of King Swegn, who had attempted to tax the men who lived in Bedericesworth contrary to their privileges, was considered to be one of St Edmund's miracles. As a result of this, Swegn's son, Cnut, became a great benefactor of both abbey and town, and he had a round stone church built to house St Edmund's remains. After its consecration in 1032, the old name Bedericesworth soon went out of use and since then St Edmund has been included in the name of the town. Benedictine monks were entrusted with the care of St Edmund's shrine.

During the reign of Edward the Confessor, the abbey received the right to mint money and was granted jurisdiction over the western part of Suffolk. (Abbots exercised considerable legal power and held their own courts.) By the time of the Norman Conquest a thriving trading community had grown up around the monastery where St Edmund's shrine lay. Pilgrims from all walks of life flocked to Bury St Edmunds.

Right:
The scene from the earliest life of St Edmund, which tells how a ferocious wolf guarded King Edmund's head, is carved on the Bishop's Throne.

Left: ⑨
An embroidery (1982) by Sybil Andrews, a local artist, which hangs in the treasury. It depicts scenes from the life of St Edmund.

A Developing Church

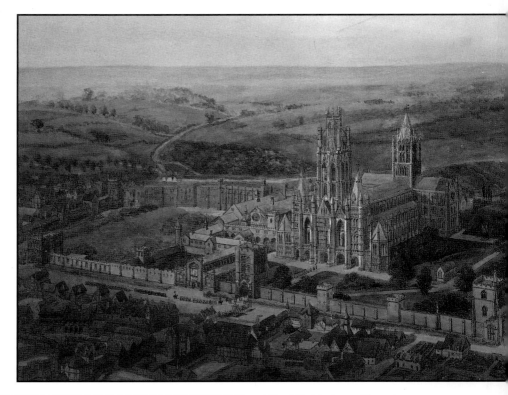

From Parish Church to Cathedral

In 1070, Arfast, Bishop of East Anglia, attempted to establish his cathedral at Bury St Edmunds. His successor, Herbert Losinga, continued the struggle against fierce opposition from the monks. Eventually, around 1096, after a few years at Thetford, Norwich became the seat of the East Anglian diocese. At the time of the Dissolution, Henry VIII contemplated establishing a see at Bury St Edmunds, with the abbey church as cathedral, but the idea never came to fruition.

At the beginning of this century there was a movement to have a diocese for Suffolk. At the time the eastern part of the county was in the Norwich diocese while the west was part of the diocese of Ely. The Diocese of St Edmundsbury and Ipswich finally came into being in 1914.

Abbot Baldwin, a Frenchman, was appointed in 1065, and he soon set about building the east end of the abbey church. He also encouraged people, French and English, to settle around the abbey, and no less than 342 houses were built nearby between 1066 and 1086. Baldwin also built a church for these people, dedicated to St Denis, because he had taken his monk's vows in Paris.

Anselm (Abbot 1121–48) resumed the building of the abbey church on a much larger scale than Baldwin had envisaged. The church of St Denis was demolished to make way for the western transept of the abbey church. Anselm replaced it with a new church, on the site of the cathedral, which he dedicated to St James, as he had hoped to make a pilgrimage to the shrine of St James at Compostella in Spain but had been frustrated by his duties in this country.

Little is known of the Norman church. William of Worcester, who visited Bury St Edmunds in 1479, suggests that it might have been about 200 feet (61m) long and 71 feet (22m) wide. Its chancel was rebuilt c.1390–1402, when bequests were made for the work. Traces of it were found in the course of excavation before the new choir was built. References to the south porch of the old church show that it also served as a chapel dedicated to Our Lady.

In 1503, work began on rebuilding the nave, but progress was very slow, the task being finished in the reign of Edward VI, who contributed towards its cost. It has been suggested that the lead remained on the nave of the abbey church until 1551 because the parishioners of St James's had to use it for their services while their own church was being rebuilt.

Below:
The Oratory Chapel,
which is reserved for
private prayer.

A brick chancel, in the classical style, was built in 1711. This, in turn, was replaced by one designed by Sir George Gilbert Scott in his restoration of the 1860s. It was at this period that the nave was given a high-pitch roof, necessitating a new gable for the west front.

The Nave

Local wills show that the present nave was begun in the summer of 1503. The mason who designed it was John Wastell who lived in nearby Crown Street. His work may also be seen in King's College Chapel, Cambridge, Bell Harry Tower at Canterbury Cathedral, the fan vault at Peterborough Cathedral and in a number of local parish churches, including Saffron Walden and Great St Mary's at Cambridge.

Many townsmen's wills include bequests towards the cost of building, and the account of John Finningham, Keeper of the Shrine of St Edmund, for 1520–21 includes a donation of 5 shillings (25p). A tablet just inside the north door records a contribution of £200 from King Edward VI, in whose reign it was completed.

The old church had stood entirely within the wall of the abbey precinct, and the new work began by building a western bay out to the street line, on a site where shops had formerly stood. Originally there were buildings close to the church on both sides at its west end, so there were no windows in its western bay. The window on the south side was created in 1850 and filled with early 16th-century glass, which had originally been in other windows. The fragments, including a Jesse tree and the story of Susanna, were once thought to be Flemish, but recent research has shown they were made in the Rouen area of France.

The carved decoration on the west front includes a scallop shell, a symbol of St James, and a chalice with a dragon on top representing St John. Wastell's west front had to be modified in the 19th century to take the high-pitch nave roof. Inside, the decoration of the western bay is richer than elsewhere.

The aisle roofs are original, but the nave roof was designed by Sir George Gilbert Scott and erected between 1862 and 1864. The colouring was begun in

Above: ③
The west end, with the font in the centre and the two Reynolds monuments on either side. The west window is Victorian, by Hardman.

1948 and completed in 1982.

The octagonal shaft on which the font stands is medieval, but the bowl and eight small shafts surrounding the old one were designed by Scott and date from 1870. The font cover is the work of F.E. Howard of Oxford and was given as a memorial to the men of the parish who were killed in the Great War. Both font and cover were coloured by the Friends of the Cathedral in 1960. The pulpit was also designed by Scott, and made by Kett.

Apart from the medieval glass in the south west window, most of the stained glass in the nave is by Clayton and Bell. A scheme was drawn up with scenes from the Old Testament on the north and from the New Testament on the

south, although the individual windows were inserted over a period of years.

A statue of Sir James Reynolds, Chief Baron of the Exchequer, who represented the town in Parliament in 1717 and died (despite what the inscription says) in 1739, and a memorial to his wife, who died in 1736, stand on either side of the west door. Many of the tablets on the north wall are connected with King Edward VI's Grammar School which was founded in 1550. The reason for this is that for many years the north aisle served as the school chapel.

Below:
The nave roof was designed by Sir George Gilbert Scott and erected between 1862 and 1864. The painting, completed in 1982, brought welcome colour into the nave.

Above:
The main hammer beams terminate with angels and shields bearing alternately the scallop shell, the wallet and the staff of St James, the crown and arrows of St Edmund and the Cross of St George.

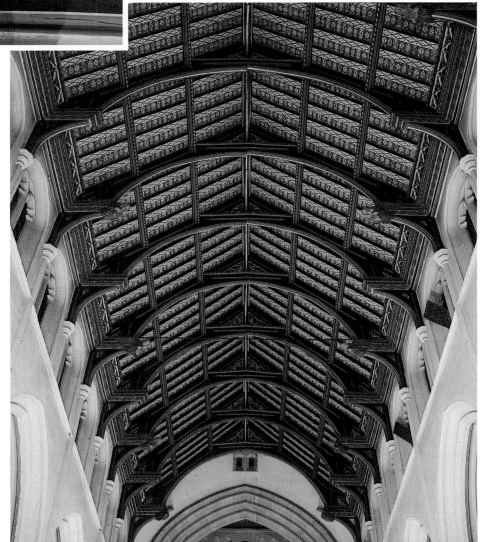

The cathedral, including the cathedral centre opened in 1990, with the abbey grounds beyond. On the right is the churchyard with its avenues of trees, some of which were planted as promenades in the 18th century. The excavated footings of the walls of the eastern arm of the abbey church show up well near the tennis courts; the easternmost apsidal chapel lies under the first tennis court, and has not been excavated. The west end of the abbey church, with houses built into it, can be seen on the right of the cathedral. The red brick house, built as Clopton's Hospital and now the Provost's House, is parallel to and close beside the south aisle of the abbey church.

The Crossing and Choir

Below: (4)
The crossing and south transept. Most of the old memorials in this church were hidden under the platform on which the pews stand when it was re-seated in the 1860s. A few tablets of special local importance are grouped on the wall of the transept.

The crossing and choir were consecrated in 1970. Scott's chancel was not large enough for cathedral services so a new east end was designed by Stephen Dykes Bower to fit the church for its new role. If required for concerts the crossing can be cleared to make space for an orchestra and choir.

Each of the stalls occupied by an honorary canon bears a name outstanding in the history of the Church in East Anglia or the abbey, or of an outstanding Christian of our own day.

Around the walls of the choir are the coats of arms of the barons appointed to enforce the terms of Magna Carta, recalling Roger of Wendover's account of a meeting of barons, said to have been held in the abbey in November 1214, when they swore to compel King John to grant them a charter of liberties.

The high altar was retained from the Scott chancel. Its altar cross was designed by W.D. Caroe and given in 1931 by Mrs John Greene in memory of an only daughter. The candlesticks were given to match the cross in 1955. To commemorate the 70th anniversary of the diocese and the cathedral in 1984, the Roman Catholic diocese of Bruges gave the large brass candlestick and the Friends of the Cathedral commissioned the 'Sun Burst' above and behind the high altar. It was designed by Stephen Dykes Bower and made in wrought iron and semi-precious stones by E. Furneaux of Great Dunnow. The high altar rails were given in memory of Richard Brook, a former bishop of the diocese.

Within the altar rails stands the feature which distinguishes a cathedral from an ordinary church, the bishop's throne, in Latin *cathedra*, which gives a cathedral its name. It was designed by F.E. Howard, and incorporates the crown

and crossed arrows of St Edmund, and carvings of the wolf guarding the saint's head, in its decoration. It was given as a memorial to the first bishop of the diocese, Dr Hodgson, who is buried within the sanctuary.

The east window of the choir contains early glass by Kempe, which used to be in the side windows of the Scott chancel. To the south of the choir is the Lady Chapel, which was furnished by the women of the diocese, with members of

the Mothers' Union contributing a great part of the cost. The sculpture of the Madonna and Child is by Leonard Goff and was given to the cathedral in 1997.

St Edmund's Chapel, on the north side, re-uses some of the fittings of the Victorian Lady Chapel, including the picture which now forms the reredos.

Throughout the cathedral there are chandeliers, also designed by Stephen Dykes Bower, and made by Eric Stevenson, a Norfolk blacksmith.

Around the Cathedral

Right: ⑦
This German painting, of about 1500, is now used as a reredos to the altar in St Edmund's Chapel.

Right: ⑦
The east window of St Edmund's chapel. The glass has been reworked from a window of *c*.1852, by Wailes, which was formerly in the east wall of the south aisle. It depicts Christ crucified, in the centre, with Our Lady and St John on either side.

Below right: ⑤
The Lady Chapel, furnished by the women of the diocese, is entered through magnificent wrought iron gates, designed by Stephen Dykes Bower and given by the Friends of the Cathedral.

Below: ⑨
Pilate washes his hands (1992), a painting by Gillian Bell-Richards, which is displayed in the treasury.

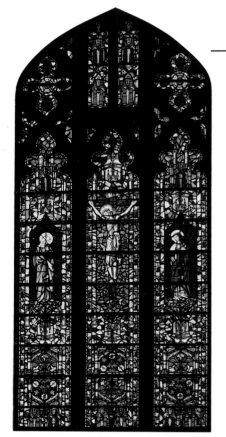

Right: ⑨
One of a pair of silver gilt flagons in the treasury, which, with an almsdish, were given to the church in 1685. Plate belonging to churches throughout the diocese is also exhibited here.

Below: ⑧
The staircase from the north transept to the treasury. An early 19th-century poor box is now used to collect the modest entrance charge, and a crucifix by the distinguished sculptor, Dame Elisabeth Frink, has recently been placed at the top of the stairs.

The Abbey

Above:
The crossing and north transept of the abbey church was built during the abbacy of Anselm, who ruled at Bury 1121–1148.

Although both St James's and St Mary's are big as parish churches go, they were small compared with the abbey church. Even after the new choir was built, the cathedral is only c.240 feet (74m) long, and St Mary's Church about 213 feet (65m); both could have been put end to end within the abbey church, which was 505 feet (155m) long.

Until the dissolution of the abbey in 1539, the sacrist was the titular parson of both parishes and appointed rather badly paid chaplains to take the services and to provide pastoral care for the parishioners. He was also responsible for the fabric of the churches and for providing the wine, candles, service books, vestments etc. required for the services.

The two fine gateways on Angel Hill are almost the only abbey buildings to have survived in their complete state. The Norman tower was designed to be a bell tower for St James's as well as the main entrance to the abbey church and it is one of the finest Norman buildings in the land. It is 86 feet (26m) high and 36 feet (11m) square with walls nearly 6 feet (2m) thick. The fine peal of ten bells was made in 1785 by recasting six old bells.

The tower was restored between 1846 and 1847 and the houses which had been built on both sides – and on the north side completely filling the space between tower and church – were

Both the medieval parish churches of the town, St James's and its neighbour, St Mary's, stood within the precinct of the abbey. By the time of Abbot Anselm, the precinct included the area which now makes up the abbey gardens and the churchyard, as well as the site of the Shire Hall and most of its main car park. On the south facing slope beyond the River Lark, the abbey had its vineyard.

On the site of the new conference centre, archaeologists found traces of an early road, with some buildings beside it and some late Saxon pottery in its ditches. This confirmed that the present Northgate Street once continued south across what became the precinct. As Abbot Anselm, who built the precinct walls and gates, also moved St James's and St Mary's to their present sites to make way for his huge abbey church, it seems likely that he extended the precinct westwards to provide sites for them.

> '*A man who saw the abbey would say verily it were a city; so many gates there are in it ... so many towers and a stately church, upon which attend three other churches also gloriously in the same churchyard, all of passing fine curious workmanship.*'
>
> JOHN LELAND c.1534

demolished. This enabled the ground to be excavated to its original level. The ground has been artificially raised in that part of the precinct, perhaps when the drainage ditch which used to run just outside the precinct was filled in at some date *c*.1730. There is a record of flooding in both St James's Church and the abbey church in 1439.

Abbot Anselm also built a gateway into the great court of the abbey (now the abbey gardens). However, this was either destroyed or very badly damaged in the course of rioting between abbey and town in 1327. Subsequently the present gateway, now known as the abbey gate, was built to replace it. The lower part was completed by 1346, but the upper parts were only finished between 1353 and *c*.1384, when John of Lavenham was the sacrist. Despite being a fine example of Decorated architecture, it was built as much for defence as ornament. On the west side arrow slits may be seen behind the niches which formerly con-

Above:
The 13th-century Abbot's Bridge, a wall rather than a genuine bridge. Planks could have been laid on this side to form a foot bridge if required. The keeper of the east gate, which stood beside the bridge, was responsible for letting down the portcullises, which prevented unauthorized entry to the abbey by water.

Left:
The abbey gate. Built after the riot of 1327 when the original Norman gate, no doubt very similar to the Norman tower, was destroyed by the townsmen.

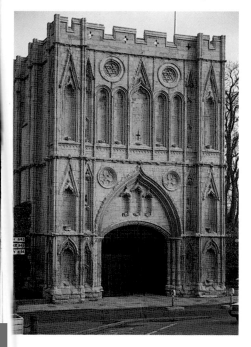

tained the figures of saints. Another notable feature of the gate is the east window, looking towards the abbot's garden and the abbey vineyard, which foreshadows the Perpendicular style of the following century. There were formerly two octagonal turrets above the stairs in the western corners of the gateway, but these became dangerous and were taken down early in the 18th century.

Above:
The Norman tower, built as a bell tower for St James's, as well as the grand entrance to the abbey church. Originally it was not detached as it is today, but was one of the entrances to the precinct.

The Cathedral Today

Cathedrals – just overlarge churches – or centres of excellence in worship mission and world outreach! St Edmundsbury Cathedral strives to be a centre of excellence in its daily offering of worship to Almighty God, and upon this foundation everything else is built. This is done on behalf of the diocese and the county, always with an eye to national and international needs, for worship needs to have a global consciousness.

Significant developments to the fabric of the cathedral have taken place in recent years with the purpose of allowing the cathedral to fulfil its role as mother church to a diocese. Between the wars, land on the north side was acquired and made easily accessible via the north-west porch of 1960. In the 1980s old vestries and temporary buildings gave way to the cathedral centre, a block adjoining the north transept. This has provided the cathedral with many amenities, including modern vestries, a well-equipped conference centre, a refectory, a treasury and a much-needed song school.

Above: ⑧
A ceiling panel from above the entrance to St Edmund's Chapel.

Below: ⑨
The cathedral centre and treasury were opened in 1990. Designed, as were most of the recent developments, by Stephen Dykes Bower, the new building gave the cathedral a song school, new vestries and conference facilities.

The consequences of this exciting development have stretched farther than the bounds of the diocese, for the cathedral is becoming increasingly a centre of pilgrimage, positioned as it is at the hub of the wheel of East Anglia and with easy access to the ports of Felixstowe and Harwich. The chaplains, stewards, vergers and the domestic facilities of our new

Above: (9)
The cathedral choir in the practice room of the new song school. Recitals and music festivals are very much part of cathedral life, and the practice room can be converted for musical performances.

Left:
A selection of the kneelers which were worked by people throughout the diocese and beyond.

Right: (9)
The refectory, as well as providing refreshment for the many 20th-century pilgrims who attend functions in the conference centre, is the place where the cathedral's own congregation gather socially between services on a Sunday morning.

building all contribute to a positive attitude and care for over 100,000 visitors every year.

Part of the ministry of the medieval abbey of Bury was its involvement in education. The cathedral centre is a worthy inheritor of this tradition. Whether it is in-service courses for clergy, training days for laity, or conferences promoted by statutory caring agencies, the cathedral is able to play its part in the development and educational health of an interesting and challenging cross-section of people.

Bury St Edmunds is blessed with an architecturally engaging building for its cathedral, well suited as a venue for the performing arts. Cathedrals nowadays are unable to be patrons of the arts in a financial sense but they can put their magnificent buildings at the disposal of the arts. Exhibitions, concerts, recitals and music festivals have become part of the pattern of the life and worship here.

Cathedrals can be seen as spiritual centres of the nation. The vibrant and challenging ministry of St Edmundsbury Cathedral means that we look forward with confidence and enthusiasm to the 21st century.